Common Sense *Solutions*

to

Real Problems

Richard Forringer

Common Sense Solutions to Real Problems
by Richard Forringer

Signalman Publishing   2011
www.signalmanpublishing.com
email: info@signalmanpublishing.com
Kissimmee, Florida

Interior layout and design by John McClure

Cover design by Joel Ramnaraine

ISBN: 978-1-935991-16-8 (paperback)
        978-1-935991-17-5 (ebook)

Library of Congress Control Number: 2011936628

Signalman
Publishing

CONTENTS

Introduction

This is a great country we live in; however, it may not be great enough. We are blessed in numerous ways that it almost defies logic. Why should we be so lucky when the great majority of the world deals with famine, a lack of potable water, inadequate housing, or child mortality rates that are beyond what we can even imagine? Yes, we have our problems, and this book will deal with my perspective on some of the most important issues that humankind faces today. Furthermore, I will bring to the table my ideas on how we can address these problems.

As a retired mathematician, I feel that my life's studies have provided me with problem solving skills that can be applied to circumstances that require critical thinking in a more creative way than has been typically applied. While some of the ideas in this book are not "new," every idea is presented in a new way. I believe the perspective and context of the arguments that I make here are unique and provide very real solutions, or partial solutions, to the problems they address. As I approach my sixty-seventh year of life, I have become increasingly aware that the number of days that I have left to do this are decreasing at a rate much faster than I care to acknowledge. Again, as a mathematician, I think about the fact that the grand total of the number of days that I have lived and the number of days that I have left to live always adds up to a constant. Many people, myself included, hope to leave something of importance behind, and this is one of my attempts to do just that. I have been fortunate to have several other projects that I have worked on to be things that I am proud of and I feel that my legacy is secure, regardless of the outcome of this book. Nevertheless, this is clearly the most aggressive attempt that I have made to make a difference on a scale much larger than previous attempts. While I really do not believe that every recommendation that I make in this book will be carried to fruition, I do believe that every one of them has potential. I must state that some of my ideas and approaches to these issues are so important that it will be extremely disappointing if they are not acted upon. Several of the ideas presented in this book are actually very simple. But, I think it is critically important to draw a distinction between what constitutes a "simple idea" and a "simplistic idea." A simple idea is one that can be enacted easily and effectively. It has the consequences intended, and those consequences are clear, specific, and measurable. A good example of a simple idea that has worked effectively is the Adopt-A-Highway (AAH) program. We have all seen the signs along the roads that state that a certain group has adopted this section of road and that it is their responsibility to keep it clean. Thousands of groups have sponsored a section of highway and the results, while not the ultimate solution, have helped. Communities have rallied behind this program—schools, church, and civic groups have done an incredible job. Furthermore, they have gained a sense of civic pride and self-respect. It has turned into a win-win situation for all involved. In my opinion, a good example of a simplistic idea would be the "Just Say No" advertising campaign to discourage drug use among children. Just Say No turned out to be an advertising campaign that was well intended and in fact probably did have some minimal results. However, those results did not meet the standard of being measurable or observable. The phrase eventually was extended to include Just Say No to pre-marital sex and other vices perceived by those who in the 80s and 90s were championed by various conservative ideologies. I am not trying to say that these well-intended ideas were unimportant or that they did not have some impact, only that they were more "simplistic" than "simple." What I am saying here is that "simple" is typically good and "simplistic" is typically not so good. Several, but not all, of the ideas presented here are indeed simple and it is my sincere hope that none are perceived as simplistic.

Each of the solutions presented are, in my

opinion, based on common sense, rather than politics or big business. They are all direct and implementable. None of them will cost massive amounts of money; many of them will save money. I believe what makes this book unique is that each of these ideas is presented in a manner that is direct, understandable, and forthright. No hidden meanings, no special interests groups are represented or consulted. Where I have *facts* I represent them as facts and where I have made assumptions, I clearly state that they are assumptions. I cannot, in all honesty, anticipate the implications of these ideas. Nor do I pretend that any of these solutions are the be-all, end-all to these problems. This is the beginning, not the end. My hope is that what I write here will stimulate thought and that discussions will be initiated because of this book.

I firmly believe that all ideas presented in this book are workable and implementable. Two things must be present for a good idea to become a real solution: One is that the idea itself must indeed be a good one. Because these are my ideas, I do have significant control over that. It is the second condition that has me concerned. Even when the idea is good and workable, it takes someone with a certain degree of power or influence to create the possibility that the idea can actually be implemented. That is where you, the reader, have a measure of control over the possibility of affecting whether the solutions are applied or not. When you read this, if you are moved to do so, I ask you to spread the word and communicate to your friends and family that this really is common sense and can make a difference in my world and your world. I do recognize that individuals and organizations have their own causes that are not represented here. I address this in a more complete manner in the last chapter. I have the greatest respect for anyone who really tries to make a difference in his or her world.

Two of my best friends in the world are actively working towards raising awareness and helping to stem the tide of young girls who are being sold as "sex-slaves." Unbeknownst to me until I became aware of their efforts, this is a worldwide problem and I certainly have the greatest respect for those who take this on as their cause. There are many very worthwhile causes that are not addressed in this book, but, as I said, this is the beginning, not the end. I do hope that what you read here, in some measure, touches your heart and is a catalyst for action on your part. It is a rare occurrence that an individual changes the world. It does happen, but it is not commonplace. On the other hand, a community of like-minded individuals has more power than you might imagine. Will you become one of these communities either adopting one of the causes that are in this book, or another that has touched your heart? Together we can make a difference! And, on a final note for this introduction, please be sure to read carefully the last chapter. It is the real key to this book becoming a success!

This book is divided into three parts, with the third part being the conclusion and summary of the material. In part one I introduce the four big problems and I present my common solutions for said problems. The issues addressed in part two are problems that can and should be addressed by individuals and small groups. Part two asks you (and me) to pick one, two, or three or more and act on it (them). I played with the notion of calling part two "The ten biggest problems with being an American." But I did not because I am confident that someone else would respond with their own idea of something that should have been included in the "biggest problems" list – and, most likely after careful reflection, I would agree. I do not pretend that this *bucket list* of ideas is, or should be, anything but my bucket list, but I do think that some (many?) of them would appear on other person's lists. But I do not present them for the purpose of comparison to what someone else may list. I present these ideas as my reflections on ten important things to think about and, to make some sort of decision concerning these ideas. It would be unrealistic to think that I will manage to address each one of these ideas in my own lifetime. Conversely, maybe this could or should be my goal?

PART I

Four Problems with Four Common Sense Solutions

CHAPTER 1

EDUCATION

Covenant Community Schools

I have spent hours and hours contemplating how to best present this idea. The content itself is not the issue for me; it is the manner in which that content is presented. I have decided to do a "cut and paste" of a paper that I wrote several years ago for a graduate course in education at Fordham University. The advantage of this is that it presents in a clear and logical format the information that I want to communicate. My professor for this course indicated in his evaluation of the paper that the material presented here was "publishable" and he encouraged me to follow up in an education journal. Instead, I have chosen to present it as part of this book. The disadvantage of presenting it in this manner is that the style is written as a research paper rather than in the same style as the rest of the book. I have decided that the advantage of clarity of an idea already written trumps the disadvantage of style. At the end of the "paper," I will include an addendum written specifically for this book.

It is clear that the system of public education in our country is in such disrepair that "typical" reform movements can no longer deal with the magnitude of the problem. The fact of the matter is, at times the problem seems so overwhelming that we as individuals and as a society have become immobilized by it. As I read thousands and thousands of pages, written by the experts in our field, I become saddened, embarrassed, and disillusioned with our inability to deal with the worsening situation. The reality, in this case, is miserable. R. Buckminster Fuller, inventor of the geodesic dome, once said, "If the future of mankind depended on who I am and what I did, who would I be and what would I do?" It is time to ask that question of ourselves. Clearly, one

paper written for a graduate course in education cannot claim to have *the* solution to these
ills. Indeed, I am convinced that there is no
one solution. Because there is "no one solution," it is easy to become apathetic. However, the lack of there being only one solution
can also be very freeing. I believe that I have
a unique proposal to make that *can* make a
difference. Something must be done. To say
we are a "nation at risk" is a massive understatement. We are more than at risk we are at
the edge of disaster. The future of our country
depends strongly on our ability to bring about
fundamental changes in… education (National Research Council, p.73). At best, our
public school system is inadequate; at worst,
it is a national tragedy. The bottom line is
the system is broken. The evidence is overwhelming. I suggest that many parents who
send their beloved children to school could be
found criminally libel for child abuse. They
are placing their children in harm's way;
possibly not literally in physical danger, yet
maybe so. Possibly not as a victim of verbal
or emotional abuse; yet, maybe so. Possibly

not in an environment where intellectual curiosity is stifled; yet, maybe so. Possibly not where creativity is dormant; yet, maybe so. But almost certainly in an environment where cooperation and caring and trust and sensitivity have nothing in common with their classroom experience. A place where more often than not the students do not want to be, where teachers do not look forward to teaching, and administrators are just trying to find a way to keep the boat afloat. In spite of thousands of dedicated and well- meaning faculty and millions of students who really *do* want to learn, it just is not working. With precious few exceptions, the system has failed us. We simply cannot give up on an entire generation! For the first time in the history of our country, our present generation will be less well educated than their parents. Toch (1991) states that the powerful language of *A Nation at Risk* and its alarming message focused national attention on public education like no other single event since Sputnik in 1957. In *A Nation at Risk* (1983) The National Commission on Excellence in Education stated the following:

Each generation of Americans has outstripped its parents in education, in literacy, and in economic attainment. For the first time in the history of our country, the education skills of one generation will not surpass, will not equal, will not even approach, those of their parents. (p. 11)

Since this report, dozens of reports have analyzed virtually every aspect of this enormous problem. All agree that the present system must change. (*A Nation at Risk*, 1983, p. 3). All the statistics, every measure of what constitutes learning, shows those scores are dropping. America is moving backward—not forward. (*A Nation at Risk,* 1983, p. 13). In 1995, SAT scores needed to be reoriented because the numbers had decreased so drastically. Heath (1984) states the decade's declining SAT scores have provoked anguished concern (p. 13). The schools are not solely to blame, but it is the schools that represent the opportunities for change.

There are some schools that are successful. Like all institutions, these schools have their problems too; yet, they are not plagued by the chronic misfortunes that persist in most schools. What is it that makes these schools different? Why do they work so much better than many others? Clearly, there is no one answer to these questions. Indeed, they have been studied and researched and "solutions" have been forthcoming. Hundreds and hundreds of books, millions of inspiring words, speeches, plays, reports, task forces, committee meetings, debates, court cases, TV talk shows, and even the pedagogical pontification of graduate students are available for study. Some of them have helped, but not many and not much. It is the basic philosophy of these "educational reforms" that I challenge. The truth we shrink from confronting is that most previous reform efforts have failed. (National Research Council, p. 77). Literally billions of dollars have been spent on this, that, or the other "plan", and while it has not been a total waste, it clearly has not worked. The history of the past 25 years of reform gives us only negative examples from which to learn (Nation Research Council p. 79). Developing clarity about what does not work is not progress. The system, as it is, fosters mediocrity. It more than contributes to it: it fosters it. The basic system lacks integrity and it is this integrity that must be restored. Under current conditions, most school teachers face nearly insurmountable obstacles (National Research Council, p. 57). There are many, many, partial and helpful suggestions or "solutions." Higher teacher salaries, better student-teacher ratio, merit pay, better benefits, more class time, less class time, bigger schools, smaller schools, raising standards, back-to-basics, tougher grading, more homework, more rigor, single sex classrooms, educate for character, magnet schools, voucher systems and so on and so on. But in and of themselves, they will not work. They cannot work. It's like trying to put frosting on a cake when the cake does not exist. The atmosphere of a school or a school system must be created from within. The good news is that it can be done. The solution is available to us. Schools must have the right to expect that regular attendance and reasonable cooperation be the norm. Students must have the opportunity to be learners in an environment where learning is prized. If a small group (or any group) of students are contributing to an environment where disruption interrupts the learning process for those students who truly want to learn, that is wrong. Schools must have the right to dismiss students that are disorderly. After all, shouldn't it be true that students' rights should apply to those who want to learn as well as those who want to disrupt learning?

So how do we do it? The key is radical structural reform. Please do not confuse radical reform with complicated reform. This can be accomplished. The basic assumptions must change. Gross (1985) states that spending billions of additional dollars on buildings, gadgets, and special programs will not do a thing (p. 261). There have been so many reports and studies that few can claim to have read them all and even fewer to have a comprehensive knowledge of what they have to say. (Gross, p. 281). I believe that most educational reform has focused on peripheral reasons for the school's failure. For the most part educational reform has been at best minimally helpful and at worst—a total failure. The cures have been simplistic, sometimes harmful, and very American—that is: new buildings, ever more money, new experimental curricula, better racial balance. The only thing we are certain of is that public education did not improve (Gross p. 211). As Sararason (1990) stated:

> Despite the vast sums of money poured into our school systems in the past twenty-five years, educational outcomes did not discernibly improve. (p. 51).

Students, parents and teachers are desperately seeking positive reform. Our students are entitled to a fair chance and they are not getting it. "... The educational foundations of our society are presently being eroded by a rising tide of mediocrity that threatens our very future as a nation" (The National Commission on Excellence in Education, 1983, p. 5). I believe that education is the major and primary foundation of our future. I also believe that continued reforms that mirror past "reforms" are doomed to the same fate as their predecessors. It is the increased dependence on external solutions that have, in my opinion, been the downfall of so many reform movements. Educational failures are too complex to be fixed by any one program or approach. However, if broadly implemented, the plan that I will put forward in this paper can have a powerful impact on the educational experiences of a wide range of students. Education in this highly complex society is exceedingly difficult. No program can claim to wipe out truancy or social inequalities or guarantee academic success; nevertheless, we have an obligation to try. The biggest risk is not taking one!

The mandate of Bucky Fuller speaks to us. Clearly I do not know that this new plan will work. I am reminded of the movie *Network* when Howard Beall stands at his window and yells, "I'm mad as hell and I'm not going to take it anymore!" I am not so much mad as I am sad. The reality of education, as we know it today, is miserable. Horror story after horror story come on the six o'clock news. The documentation of the failure of our schools is rampant. Just ask the cop at the door. Traditional schools tend to put academic <u>achievement</u> as the <u>purpose</u> of their existence rather than the <u>result</u> of their being. This is where my suggested reform differs from the norm. A school that focuses on building strength of intellect while ignoring strength of character is bound to fail. Reform that does not take this into account is not only ineffective, but it is also foolish and wasteful. It is the structure itself that needs to be addressed and is what I believe the notion of a COVENANT school does. This is not a quick fix. It will solve some, but not all of the problems. Provisions must be made for those students who do not respond to the notion of a COVENANT COMMUNITY SCHOOL.

So, what is a COVENANT COMMUNITY SCHOOL (henceforth referred to as CCS) and how does it work? Simply put, it is an adjunct to the present school system. My proposal is that each public school system makes available for <u>all</u> students the opportunity to attend a school where the primary driving force is the student's own commitment to discipline, self-respect, and the universal values of honesty, trust, compassion, and responsibility for one's own actions. These values are so basic that they define what it means to be human. They encompass all persons: young and old, black and white, male and female, academically gifted and academically challenged. It will be each student's responsibility to accept reasonable rules and the consequences of his or her own behavior, or attend one of the non-CCS public schools. After all, that is what kids are attending now. This is, in reality, an option that is added to their current choices. It is an opportunity that is open to everyone. No fees. No restrictions based on previous academic or social history. There is no tie to academic ability or success. CCS will equally benefit the academically talented and the academically challenged. Many schools already have academically talented classes. That is good. Many schools already have special classes for students whose academic orientation is below average. That is good. Instituting a CCS will have no negative impact on those programs. It will strengthen them. To apply to become a member of a CCS, a student would complete an application form and write a statement of his or her own indicating his/her desire to be a part of this program. Students want to be a part of something that is successful. Every student that completes this process with a minimum degree of purposefulness will become a member of the school. I have reluctantly attached in the appendix an example of what a CCS application form might look like. I say reluctantly because I believe the process should be a local one with each system establishing its own standards and requirements. The CCS must provide clear, significant, appropriate and achievable behavioral and ethical expectations for their students. The guidelines of the covenant are binding. This is the code of ethics and behavior that is the standard by which each individual's participation is based. If someone is unable or unwilling to live within the stated parameters of the covenant, then they are not maintaining the purpose for which the community was formed. You do have a choice—behave, be respectful, follow the rules, be courteous—or go to school elsewhere. Clearly, an imperative would be that other options are available. Students who choose violence and disruption on school grounds are not welcome. Students who rebel against the rights of others must be removed from the campus. The key is that the students are responsible for their own actions. As disruptive behavior breeds disruptive behavior, so too does caring breed caring. If a student does not value their right to a free education, then they should not be allowed to ruin it for others. Students who try their best day in and day out deserve the opportunity to be the best they can be without having to put up with those people who do not care. Clearly, each of us in this community—adults and students—is human—thus prone to making mistakes. It must be the purpose of the CCS system to work with members of the community and to guide them along the way. When we stumble, there must be caring persons there to keep us from falling, or to pick us up when we fall. And fall we will. Such is our nature. However, once it is established that the student wants to participate in this venture and the school responds favorably, then the CCS is committed to helping that student keep his/her covenant. Sadly, there will be times when it is necessary to dismiss a student from a CCS. The key factor will be: "Is this student's actions interfering with *other* students' opportunities to learn?" That is what is happening now in so many classrooms. The CCS will not tolerate disruptive behavior that infringes on the rights of *other* students. Those students who want to be in the classroom where learning can take place will have that opportunity. The great majority of people are capable of solid citizenship if they know what is expected of them. It is true that there are a small percentage of students in the United States who are beyond mischievous. They are unable or unwilling to be cooperative within a reasonable system's expectations. The CCS must have the opportunity to work without them, if necessary. This system can only work if great care and thought is given to helping students who, for one reason or another, do not, (will not, cannot, choose not), function in a classroom in ways that meet with the community's covenant. I believe that fewer and fewer students will choose that option when schools finally start to provide an environment where learning can take place. All students who are willing to accept their end of the bargain are welcome to the CCS classroom. It is so logical, sensible, and reasonable—a simple, yet profound notion. There is no reason not to follow up on such a proposal. It is a win-win situation. I believe it is also imperative that the application process be updated yearly and that students have a primary voice in that process.

A key to the success of the CCS is that *every* school within a given system makes this option available. Systems don't change easily. Forces acting to keep a system at rest are in place and are resistant to external pressure. Usually a multitude of catalysts must be present to stir things up enough to impact an institution—especially one as large and pervasive as the public school system. We all know it does not work, but without something to replace it, we are helpless. One day comes, and then the next and on and on. The longer we learn to live with this unbelievably incompetent system the less unbelievable it appears. Kopp (1972) suggests that the misery of the known is more acceptable to us than the potential vitality of the unknown (p. 4). The same dynamic is present in our lives whenever change is an option. It is a primary reason why alcoholism, abuse, dysfunctional families, and addictive behaviors (smoking, overeating, drugs) continue without resolution. Without the hope of a better option, things will stay the same or get worse. If you do not know what your other options might be, then the option you are living with—as bad as it may be—will continue until there is a crisis (death, divorce, DWI) or an external force (lawyer, judge, guru, therapist, spouse, child, faith) intervenes in a way that can impact the circumstances. External forces have been abundant in education—each offering their own form of hope—usually expensive and based on a theory of education that is unproven and/or untested. It is in these two respects that the CCS system is so dramatically different. The administration and clerical expense would be minimal compared to previous reform movements. The fundamental principle upon which the system is based is functioning now. That fundamental principle is *choice*. Lieberman (1989) equates "choice" with a voucher system (p. 152). CCS suggests that "choice" does *not* merge private and public institutions into a common system. Independent schools now offer choice to those who are willing and able to pay for it. CCS would offer choice to *all* students. Open to everyone who is willing to make their covenant, their solemn pledge, to stand up and be counted among those who will make a difference in their own world— in my world— in your world! Reform of any nature that does not include structural change of the system is, in my opinion, doomed to fail. Under current conditions the obstacles are insurmountable. I am not suggesting that the CCS system is the only solution. However, I am suggesting that only reform that includes choice and adherence to clearly stated expectations will have a chance of impacting our current dysfunctional public school system.

Teacher assistants

Remembering that the title of this book is ***Common Sense Solutions to Real Problems,*** I offer the following direct and simple recommendation that will help solve three very important problems in our economy today.

As of today, there are thousands of unemployed teachers who have lost their jobs because local school districts just cannot afford to keep them. Our federal government has enacted emergency measures to bail out banks and loan institutions and other financial organizations. This "bailout" was expensive, but, I believe, important and neccssary. The problem was that the great sums of money went to institutions that had used bad judgment and gotten themselves into financial difficulties. The government needed to step in and "save" them in order to stabilize the economy and not allow a recession to become a depression. Thank you! I am not arguing that this was a bad move, or that it did not need to be done. It was unfortunate, and an enormous expense, but you have to do what you have to do and important and powerful people made those difficult decisions. They had the information and I believe they acted in the best interests of the country. But, what is amazing to me is that that same option is open to another institution and it has not been forthcoming.

If the government can come up with a "stimulus package" to bail out the previously mentioned institutions, then it seems reasonable that the same source of funds could be used to hire teachers and relieve not only the near double-digit unemployment rate, but also provide more and better help in each classroom. As mentioned earlier in this chapter, our current educational system is in need of some drastic help. Clearly, having two teachers in every classroom would provide opportunities that are currently unavailable. One of the mantras of the economic struggle that we have been going through has been that we need to put people back to work to stimulate the economy. Working people pay taxes. Working people buy cars. Working people take more vacations. Certainly, houses that would otherwise be foreclosed upon would be saved if more people were working. Again, it is a win-win situation. Dollar for dollar, this would be money well spent. The reasoning behind spending millions and millions of dollars on projects that will create a few jobs as opposed to millions and millions of dollars that will go directly for job creation seems to present a clear choice. While there would be some overhead expenses with a project such as this, they would be minimal compared to the costs for those other options currently being considered. For every $35,000 spent, I would guess that a $30,000 job could be created. That is by far a better bang for your buck than anything else that is being considered for spending stimulus money. That person who is getting a $30,000 teaching position would be paying taxes, rather than receiving unemployment and would be spending money that would encourage other small business owners.

In the first paragraph of this chapter, I stated that this solution would help to solve three very important problems. What are they? First, it would lower the unemployment rate. Second, it would strengthen our schools. Third, it would stimulate the economy. What are the downsides? Well, the money to fund this project would have to come from somewhere. The good news is that the government has already set aside plenty of stimulus money to fund this and several other projects. The key is a question of what priority comes first. (Or even second, third, or fourth!)

CHAPTER 2

ENERGY

Speed limits

Ten years ago I was diagnosed with type 2 diabetes. To make a long story short, after the initial shock, concern, and worry, I spent several months studying and learning all I could about just what that meant for my family and me. I recall vividly one thing that my Doctor said to me that at the time surprised me, but now makes all the sense in the world. She said that she sometimes wished she could lie to a few of her patients and tell them that they had diabetes, because if you take it seriously (which, of course, many people do) it means a pretty significant change in your life style. For me, I have made changes in how I eat, how I exercise, and I have a greater awareness of my general health. Don't get me wrong, I wish I did not have diabetes, but I sure am glad that I now take better care of myself and I actually feel much better now than I did prior to the diagnosis. The point of all this is that I have realized by this, and other events, that it is not always the good news that is the catalyst for change. My Mom taught me to play bridge and I recall her saying that it is often how you play your bad hands that shows your skills as a bridge player, rather than how you play the good ones. This is, in part, how I feel about this chapter of this book. My responsibility to myself as the author is to somehow convince my readers that there is a "bad hand" that needs to be played well, or that there is a difficult diagnosis that needs to be responded to in a manner that will make the best of a bad situation. This will not be easy! Both of these examples say to me that sometimes I need to do the right thing, even if it is hard or unfortunate or not what I wish for. Dealing with Diabetes and playing the bad hands are sometimes what life puts in our path. You just have to do what you have to do. Not all decisions are happy ones, easy ones, or popular ones, but you do what you have to do because the alternative is unacceptable. This logic, this reasoning, this process of coming to a decision sometimes takes more energy and more resolve than one would wish for, but that is often what life is all about. Let me ask you to think about the following question really seriously. If you were faced with making an unpopular decision, but it would literally save thousands and thousands of lives and the only downside would is that it would be inconvenient to some people, would you do it? Of course, you want more information, but I am confident that your first inclination is to say yes, you would! Remember, the premise of this book is common sense solutions to real problems. I am, in an absolute sense, convinced that the very unpopular and difficult decision to lower the national speed limit to 55 mph is the right thing to do. The up sides are enormous! The down sides are, relatively speaking, trivial! Yet, as much as it has been talked about, debated, and considered, it has not been done. Why? Because it is politically incorrect. In my mind, that is the most stupid and idiotic and immature reasoning that one could take. What? Are you kidding me? Is it really true that politicians are unwilling to make that unpopular decision because they might lose a few votes or that they might raise the ire of a significant group of people? Now is the time to do what is right even if it is unpopular. I would guess, of course, that there are a significant number of people who are not convinced that it is indeed the right thing to do. My goal is to convince them otherwise. On the one hand, it won't be easy. On the other hand it could be if those who oppose the idea are open minded enough to really think this through and consider all of the pros and cons. In my mind, the pros outweigh the cons by such a dramatic degree, that eventually the decision will be made and the country will be dramatically better off for it! I do know, of course, that there will still be many people who oppose this idea, but it is my hope that those of us who do come to the conclusion that it should happen will create a unified voice that will be heard by those empowered to make such decisions. I must admit that I am not so bold or egotistical to believe that I have *the* solution that needs to be enacted, but I am determined enough to present it and see what happens.

No doubt, someone by now has noticed that the title of this chapter is "Energy", and thus far there has been nothing written that seems to have much of anything to do with energy. I was twenty-nine in 1974 when Richard Nixon, in response to the Saudi Oil embargo that created a major energy crisis, made the decision to lower the speed limits to 55 mph. This speed limit stayed in effect for twenty-one years. For the life of me, I just can't figure out why it changed back to the way it is today. Here is another example of a simple solution that is not simplistic. We know it will work because it has worked. The costs involved in enacting this legislation are minimal. It is not the only solution nor is it the single best solution. But in my mind, the United States will not have a comprehensive energy strategy unless we are willing to consider other possible avenues for conservation than the ones now being considered. For one thing, most of the current plans being considered are long range and expensive. I do not discourage long range and expensive plans, but I do wonder why they would preempt immediate short-range plans that will make a dramatic and significant difference. It just doesn't make sense. Remember— "common sense solutions to real problems" is what this is all about. Can someone — anyone—explain the down side to this move? I do know there are some legitimate concerns, but when weighed against the energy savings and the thousands of lives that will not be lost due to high-speed crashes, the conclusion seems obvious. Some estimates state that up to four thousand deaths per year were avoided purely because of lowering the speed limit for the twenty-one years between 1974 and 1985. Think about that. If you were in a position to make a decision that could save lives and the primary reason you do not make that decision is because some people want to drive faster, does that make any sense at all? Of course not! I certainly know that the arguments that I make in this chapter are not new and this has been considered over and over in response to the higher costs of gasoline, but just because the ideas have been rejected in the past does not mean that that rejection was the right decision. In fact, it was not. It is not! You might be able to tell that I feel adamantly about this. What if one of the lives saved is one of your loved ones? How could you possibly live with yourself if you knew that you could have done the right thing and you didn't? There are certain trains of thought that are just bizarrely strange to me. Will we not lower the speed limit for a fear that the driving public will just ignore the limits and drive faster anyway? That is bizarre! There are multiple excellent reasons for making this change and just a few (stupid, in my mind) reasons for not making this change. Let me list, in order, what I consider the three most important reasons for lowering the speed limits on major highways to 55 mph.

1) The death tolls on highways will decrease dramatically. The statistics

are undeniable. Lives will be lost if we don't take this step. For every day that we continue to wait, an average of ten people will die who would have not died if we had enacted this change. I wonder why it is necessary to even go on to other reasons, when this one is so dramatic and significant and convincing that it really does suffice to make the decision justifiable! We not only need to do this, we need to do it as soon as possible. Waiting costs lives!

2) A comprehensive energy policy must include a wide range of plans and policies and perspectives. Again, the statistics are overwhelming! While estimates vary as to precisely how much gas will be saved because of driving at this lower speed, no one denies that the savings are significant. Our dependence on foreign oil needs addressed with multiple plans. This one can be enacted quickly and easily and with minimal expense. We

indeed could immediately decrease our dependence on foreign oil with a stroke of the pen!

3) If one averages 55 mph on a 550-mile trip, it will take 10 hours. If one averages 60 miles per hour on a 550-mile trip it will take 9 hours and 10 minutes. If one averages 65 mph on a 550-mile trip, it will take approximately 8 and a half hours. And, let's face it, even when the speed limit is 65, one does not really "average" that speed. So, the bottom line is that a full day's trip might take an hour to an hour and a half longer. Is that worth the increased probability of a lost life? Of course not! People who commute 50 or 60 miles one way to work will take 5 to 10 minutes longer to get to work, but their probability of actually getting there has increased! If three times every month a plane with 100 people on it crashed and killed everyone on board, wouldn't you reconsider flying? Wouldn't you

expect your government to look into it and try to figure out some way of minimizing the carnage? The equivalent of that is happening on the highways every month of every year. Now is the time to do something about that! We absolutely must increase the awareness of this national tragedy!

Traffic Lights

How many times have you sat at a red light at ten o'clock in the evening on some semi-deserted road and just waited while no one came from your left or from your right? Fact of the matter is that it happens all the time. A friend of mine once joked that a red light in the middle of the morning is just a recommendation. What I really do not understand is why and how decisions are made to change certain intersections from "normal" red/green lights to blinking red/green lights. What I do understand is that it just is not done often enough and this relatively minor change would save time, energy, aggravation, and money. I have lived in the same town for the past forty-two years and I have a very good knowledge of the traffic patterns and where and when traffic lights are meaningful in the late evening or middle of the night or before "rush hour" in the morning. Fact of the matter is that gallons of gasoline and hours of time are wasted because our community does not have flashing red/green lights at the appropriate places at the appropriate times. Multiply that by thousands and thousands and the savings is huge. Remember, we are talking big numbers here. There are tens of thousands of cars driving in small to medium cities during hours when traffic lights are meaningless. Actually, they are not meaningless, they are very meaningful but in a very bad way. I don't know how to estimate how many thousands of gallons of gasoline are wasted every day, but common sense would indicate that the savings would be significant. Again, we are talking about a change that is easy to implement and that there is virtually no reason not to do it. I am not an expert on how cars work or what makes for good or bad gas mileage, but I am more well-read on the subject than most people and it is not a topic that takes a person with a PhD in physics to understand. But, just in case, I did consult with a friend who has his doctorate in physics and he confirmed that indeed the obvious truth is the same as the actual truth. There is no doubt in his mind (or my mind) that this reasonable and relatively simple (but not simplistic) change would be one of the things we can and should do that would make a very real difference in the amount of gasoline consumed each day. Now, I am not a physicist, but I am a mathematician, and I do understand the power of numbers and the impact of many small changes. Can you imagine if each one of us were able to save just a half a gallon of gasoline a month what the cumulative impact of that would be? It is staggering. So, here is a meaningful and simple change that would make a significant difference in our dependence on foreign oil. I understand and appreciate the many plans and goals of those who are charged with making long-range energy decisions. What I don't understand is the seeming unwilling-ness to embrace common sense solutions that are there in front of them.

CHAPTER 3

THE WAR ON DRUGS

Before I get into my common sense reasons why our current policies about drug use are great examples of uncommon sense, let me state in no uncertain terms that I am against the use of marijuana and cocaine and that group of other drugs that are now illegal. I do not want to encourage anyone to use these drugs. It is my opinion that these drugs are bad things. I feel the same way about alcohol and tobacco. What this chapter is about is how we, as a nation, deal with drug and alcohol and tobacco use. I believe that what we are doing now makes so little sense that the only reasonable thing to do is to change our current strategy. When what you are doing is not working then do something different. Is there anyone who thinks what we are currently doing is good? I don't think so. I am convinced that the single major difficulty is not agreement or disagreement that our current approach is not working, but agreement or disagreement about how to change our current strategy. So, if we can agree that our current policies are not working then at least that is a good start. If we can agree that the laws as they current exist are fundamentally broken, then at least that is a good start. If we can agree that we are failing in what we would like to be doing, then at least that is a good start. But, all of these good starts will be meaningless unless we as a nation can really come up with some common sense solutions to replace the failed strategies of the past. It has been over forty years since President Nixon first declared that there needed to be a War on Drugs and asked Congress for $155 million to combat a problem that he deemed (forty years ago) to be a national emergency. In these past forty years, the problem has just gotten worse. Forty years of a failed policy is enough. There are some things that seem so obvious that it defies a person's imagination as to how anyone could not see it. Continuing along the same path just makes no sense at all! I believe that change will not occur unless there is agreement that change needs to occur. I will not, in this chapter, spend too much time and energy explaining why change needs to occur. Yet, I will outline what in my opinion are the major reasons why our current policies are ineffective and the conclusion that they need to change will, I believe, be obvious. Fact of the matter is that drugs are bad for you. Fact of the matter is that alcohol and tobacco products are vices. Any solution will not solve that problem. Which is worse: alcohol products or marijuana? Which is worse: tobacco products or alcohol? Which is worse: tobacco products or marijuana? Actually, three pretty good questions. Each is bad. There is no doubt about that. Yet, our country has chosen three very different approaches to dealing with these problems as far as the legal system is concerned. We once attempted prohibition (alcohol), which an abject failure. In fact, it was such a failure that it now stands alone as the only example of a United States Constitution amendment to be repealed. The laws that currently are in place against marijuana use are, for all practical purposes, the same laws that once were a part of our constitution. It was from 1920-1933, illegal to manufacture, sell, or transport liquor. It is, today, illegal to manufacture, sell, or transport marijuana. Now, I know that there are variations of these laws from state to state, but, for all practical purposes, we currently are under a "prohibition" when it comes to the use of marijuana.

I stated in the previous paragraph that I would not make a big deal out of the why of our current laws not working, and that there was general acceptance that what we are currently doing is not working, but I must at least mention what I consider the four big reasons to modify our current strategies.

1) The jails and prisons in the United States are packed with people who have committed crimes that are directly or indirectly associated with drugs.

2) The United States has provided a cottage industry for the illegal production and distribution of drugs. There are no reliable statistics that can include the number of people whose lives have been ruined because of the illegal trafficking of drugs. However, there is widespread agreement that whatever that number is, it is massive and growing.

3) Not only have our current laws not provided the intended results, they have been counterproductive and have actually created more vast networks of organized crime. In short, they have created more problems than they have solved, just as the period of prohibition did in the 1920s.

4) The financial burdens to our budget are staggering. If we taxed drugs that were made legal in the same way that we tax cigarettes and alcohol, we could provide additional billions of dollars to our economy. If we stopped putting

people in jail or prison for drug use or possession or trafficking, the jail population would drop dramatically and the costs of incarceration would drop. The total of all these savings over a period of years would be hundreds of billions of dollars!

So enough of the "what is wrong and why is it wrong" and on to the "what can be done about it" part of this chapter. Please note that I am not saying that this is the only solution or that it should be brought into fruition is the exact manner that I prescribe here, but I am saying that any and every solution must include these basic principles. Nor am I saying that things will be all better if we do something different than what we are doing now. But I am saying that things will be improved. Perhaps still bad, but at least improved. It is my opinion that we will never legislate our way out of a drug problem, just as we have been unable to legislate our way out of an alcohol or tobacco misuse. However, there are three things that *must* be done to put us on the right track. I will list each and then expand on the reasoning.

1) Decriminalize drug production, sales, and use.

2) Treat drug abuse as a medical problem, not a legal problem.

3) Education, not legislation, is the solution.

Let's take them one at a time. First, decriminalization has been a notion that has been tossed around for years. The so-called "soft" drugs like marijuana should not and cannot be considered in the same light as crack cocaine, opium, heroin, or other "hard" drugs. Just what constitutes a "soft" drug or a "hard" drug is a question for doctors, not mathematicians (like me). Marijuana should be sold and taxed in the same manner as cigarettes. Crack cocaine, heroin, opium and the other hard drugs should be available by prescription only, so the addict will have an option to get a hold of these drugs legally, without having to resort to criminal acts. On December 5th, 1933 the 21st amendment was passed repealing the 18th amendment—prohibition.

Almost instantaneously, speakeasies disappeared. Mobsters and crime took a totally different look with the repeal of prohibition. It was a new world! The same will happen when the laws against manufacture, selling, distributing and use of marijuana are thrown out. Without the need to break the law to use drugs, there will be a totally different approach to drug use. A wave of criminal activities will cease! The war on drugs will take on a new meaning. It will no longer be fought (and lost) in the courts but in schools and homes and newspapers. Certainly there will be reasonable and appropriate restrictions on the use of marijuana, just as there are reasonable and appropriate restrictions on the use of tobacco products and alcohol. But no longer will we be incarcerating citizens for buying, selling, or using soft drugs such as marijuana. Like cigarettes and beer, it will no longer be a criminal offense.

Alcoholism was a problem before, during, and after prohibition. There is disagreement about how much better or worse it became when prohibition was repealed. Drug addiction was a problem years ago, it is a problem now, and it will continue to be a problem after decriminalization of soft drugs. I am sure there will be disagreement as to how much better or worse it is going to be after the laws change. One thing is certain, however, and that is decriminalization of soft drugs will remove the problems from the courts and replace them where they belong, with social, educational, and medical professionals. I think I need to state here as clearly as I know how that the use of alcohol and the use of drugs (even soft drugs) and the use of tobacco products is a scourge on society. We must do everything we can to minimize the use of these terrible products, especially by young people. One might reasonably ask, "Then why are you advocating for legalization?" It's a fair question that deserves a strong response. Making drugs illegal doesn't work. Prohibition against drugs has created more problems than it has solved. You just cannot legislate morality or good judgment. In fact, legislation has the opposite effect. I want to decriminalize drug use to give us the chance to fight the war on drugs in an arena where it can be won. Decriminalizing drug use will drastically reduce crime and improve health. I do realize that arguments both for and against drug being legalized are controversial. I am concerned that the controversy is primarily a function of preconceived notions and that logical common sense thinking has a hard time convincing a person who has his or her mind already made up. Of course, one could make the reasonable argument that those of us who believe otherwise also have our own preconceived notions and we too are subject to not being open to another person's view of what common sense is.

Decriminalizing drug production, sales, and use is not enough. We must start a new war on drugs that has nothing to do with the law and has everything to do with a humanistic approach to the problem. Doctors, not lawyers, need to develop strategies to minimize drug use and abuse. Realistically, there are certain facts that just cannot be denied. Alcoholism is a disease that will be with us forever. We can work hard at decreasing the spread and impacts of the disease, but we cannot irradiate it. In like manner, drug use and abuse will continue despite every attempt to cure the problem. The good news is that we can, with the right tools, minimize the horrible impacts of these diseases as we become more educated about proper treatments. I believe it is sad, but true, that we are not in the "modern age" of medicine when it comes to treatments available for addictions. Yet, we are making slow progress. By treating these problems as diseases and not crimes, the opportunities for treatments improves and the time will come when we see remarkable progress towards creating a world where drug and alcohol abuse is dramatically less than it is currently.

Third, and finally, the absolute key to fighting the war on drugs is education, not legislation. The perfect example is what has happened in our society to the perception and use of cigarettes during the past forty years. To say it is dramatic is an understatement of enormous proportion. When I was a kid smoking was considered cool and sexy. The great majority of teenagers thought smoking was "fun" and it was as natural as French fries at McDonalds. You could not turn on the TV or go to a movie without seeing someone smoking. It was—literally—everywhere. So what happened? What changed? Why is it different for teenagers today? There are multiple answers, but clearly the biggest one is education. No one can predict with certainty what the future will bring, but it certainly seems more than just highly plausible that the future of drug use can have a similar outcome to the events that have led to the drastic reduction of smoking. At the age of eighteen, I smoked two packs a day. I continued to smoke for twenty years, but eventually I quit because it became clear to me that quitting was the right thing to do. I did not quit because the government passed laws that made smoking illegal! While I was never a heavy drinker, I also quit drinking about the same time. I cannot say precisely why I quit smoking and drinking, but I can say that it was a personal decision based on reasoning, thinking, and personal growth. I am somewhat embarrassed that it took me so long and I am not proud of the fact that that I started in the first place. Yet, in the 1960s it just was not that big of a deal. It is now and I am glad. It should be! However, let us not forget that during this radical change in values (as related to cigarette use) no one ever spent one day in prison because he or she purchased or sold cigarettes. Education was and is the key. Warning labels on packs of cigarettes has helped. Banning the use of advertisement on television and in magazines has helped. An increased awareness of the medical problems associated with the use of tobacco products has helped. Children's urging their parents to stop smoking has helped. There literally are dozens of reasons why the number of persons who smoke has declined, but they are all associated with education and medical factors, not laws that prohibited the use of tobacco products. Now, I do know that there are laws associated with the age that minors are allowed to purchase alcohol and tobacco products. These are not laws that result in incarceration or that leads to crime sprees, however. They are common sense rules as opposed to big-brother laws! I did not quit smoking because I had to; I quit because I chose to! I made the decision to stop drinking because it was wise, not because it was forced upon me by the laws that punish a person for making a bad decision. It is just as impossible to legislate morality in society as it is to legislate kindness or good manners. People make good decisions because they realize the need to do so, not because they are told or forced or because laws are passed. That is not to say that all laws are bad or that we should not be held accountable for those times when we do something that is illegal. But the laws must focus on rules of society that apply to such things as safety and protection, not attempting to legislate morality.

It is fine for the government to tell me that I can't drive while intoxicated, but it is not fine for the government to tell us that we can't use alcohol. It is fine for the government to tell us that we can't drive 75 mph in a school zone because it is a question of the safety of our children. There are many laws that are sensible and there are other laws that are not. Then, there are those laws that fall somewhere in between sensible and not sensible. Those are the gray areas where our legislators must make some difficult decisions. I am so very glad that many of those are left up to the states and not the federal government.

The law in North Carolina tells me that I cannot drive my motorcycle without wearing a helmet. If I lived in Ohio, I have the option of not wearing a helmet. There is reasonable debate as to whether or not these kinds of things should be legislated. To be frank, I just don't know. Most laws of this nature are not very important to most people. But, it is certainly true that there are differences from one state to another that could cause a person to make the decision to live in a state whose laws about abortion or adoption by gay or lesbian couples or specific tax rules that impact retirement or savings or income. Fortunately, those are issues for another person in another book at another time. They are certainly real and they are important.

CHAPTER 4

THE FEDERAL BUDGET

Similar to our failing school systems, there is no doubt that we are living in a time of a budget fiasco. Both are problems that get talked about and that are in the news almost daily, but for years and years, the problems just keep getting worse. We are not only *not* solving the problems; they are getting worse every day. I have already dealt with my "common sense solutions" relative to education, and this chapter will deal with the Budget Crisis. And there is no doubt that it is indeed a crisis. One cannot overemphasize just how horrific this problem is. In April of 2011, the House of Representatives, the Senate and the President spent hours and hours and days wasted on arguing about a miniscule percentage of the budget in an attempt to avoid the government shutting down. They succeeded... Sort of... But at what price? The rest of this chapter will deal with what I believe to be a unique and common sense approach to the problem that will really work. Unlike what has happened over the years that the budget has caromed out of control, there is hope for better days ahead, but more of the same old political solutions are not the answer.

Like many professional areas, most of us have a minimal understanding of medicine and automotive repairs and mathematics, but that minimal understanding does not qualify us to be doctors or mechanics or mathematicians. I have no problem putting ice on a sprain or bandages on a cut or taking Aspirin for a headache, but I will call on a professional if I need surgery! I have no problem putting air in a tire that is low, or changing my oil, or replacing my windshield wipers, but if my transmission needs rebuilt, I will call on a qualified mechanic. I have no problem figuring out how much change to get from a twenty-dollar bill when I spend

$12.30, or doing my federal or state taxes, or using a calculator, but when I need to use calculus or multivariable equations, I call on a mathematician. Why then, do you suppose, that well-meaning and well-qualified politicians think that they have the skills to attack a mathematical problem like a complex budget that requires skills that they just do not have? It is my opinion that people who do not have the skills to solve it cannot solve the problem! If we don't want our Senators doing heart surgery or rebuilding a carburetor, then what makes us think that we want them fixing a budget? As much as they might want to be able to do any of these things, they have enough sense not to try to do some of them because they are unqualified to do so. I am saying here in an absolute sense, that politicians are not capable of the mathematics necessary to fix a complicated budget any more than they are capable of surgery. If you think carefully about this, I am confident that you will agree. But, nevertheless, I will give some obvious reasons why this must in fact be true. All of you non-mathematicians out there who are reading this consider your own understanding of the figures that are used in the Federal Budget. Do you think you really have a *clear* understanding of the differences among a million and a billion and a trillion? I refer to them as the "M" word and the "B" word and the "T" word. Many non-mathematicians use these words semi-interchangeably. How absurd; and I know of what I speak, as I am a mathematician. In undergraduate school, I majored in mathematics. I earned a Master's in Education where I focused my energy on the teaching of mathematics. I taught algebra and beyond for forty-two years before I retired, I have published three peer-reviewed articles in a major math journal, I have had ten original problems published in the calendar of problems section of the *Mathematics Teacher*, and I have written a book (yet unpublished) on *The Binomial Expansion and Symbolic Logic.* Having said that, I would state in no uncertain terms that I do not have the skills that I need to tackle a problem like the federal budget. But, I certainly have the skills to understand that it takes a mathematical approach to have any chance of experiencing success! I know enough to know that I do not know enough! Just as I would not want my dermatologist to do open heart surgery, I would not want a mathematician with my credentials to work on the budget. However, I do trust my dermatologist and know that she recognizes the limits of her expertise and will only practice the medicine she is qualified to practice. As a mathematician, I recognize my own limits and will use my expertise to only perform the mathematical tasks for which I am qualified. If I, as a qualified mathematician, am willing to acknowledge my limits as to how to solve the budget crisis, does it not seem reasonable that a politician would also recognize his or her own limitations in this area? I admire and respect those who are willing to run for public office and accept the challenges of the political arena. What I do not admire or respect is the notion that they are willing to try to do open-heart surgery when they are unqualified or when they might try to rebuild a transmission when they just don't know how. Oh, wait a minute… I guess they really don't do those silly things! So can anyone tell me why he or she feels qualified to do the job of a professional mathematician when they just are not? Fact of the matter is, that no matter how dedicated and earnest and caring they may be, every time they attempt open-heart surgery they would fail. And, they know that, so to their credit they just do not try. Fact of the matter is, every time they attempt to fix a very broken budget, they will fail, and sadly, they keep trying anyway. We must get them to recognize and accept their limitations! I would go so far as to say that any member of the House or Senate who does not understand that should not be there! There is nothing wrong with my dermatologist because she cannot perform open-heart surgery, and there is nothing "wrong" with my Senator just because she cannot muster up the mathematical skills to fix the budget. She, and her peers, must accept that there are limitations to their abilities and hand the ball over to those people who are qualified. The budget will never be fixed until they do that. In the Senate of the United States we have one hundred well-qualified and dedicated politicians. One might even say they are brilliant people to have gotten to where they are. Most (maybe all) are dedicated public servants who really do want to make our country a better place. But, how many of them understand what to do to make our budget work? The obvious answer is: "none." Or, if they do they have failed miserably at enacting their ideas to make things better. The system is as broken as broken can be. I believe that, without a change in strategy, there is no hope of things getting better. More of the same unworkable solutions will result in more of the same unworkable outcomes. There is hope, but it does not lie within the structure that currently exists.

I believe the following hypothetical story will illustrate an important concept that our legislators don't seem to be grasping. It does not take a skilled mathematician to see the flaws in the logic of this story, so I wonder why the budget committees in the House of Representatives and the Senate have not noticed that the same dynamic as is illustrated

in this story are also—though on a much larger scale, illustrated in their reasoning (or lack
thereof).

Suppose a power company comes up with
a payment plan that works like this. A family
agrees to pay a specific amount each month, regardless of how much energy they have used.
This saves the power company the time, trou-
ble, and costs of reading a meter each month,
and allows the customer to have a more stable
budget. If, at the end of the year, the customer
has paid too much, a refund will be made. If,
at the end of the year, the customer has paid
too little, then the monthly payment will be
recalculated and adjusted for the following
year. Therefore, a customer agrees and pays
$150 a month for the first year and all is fine.
Unfortunately, at the end of the first year two
very bad things happen. The customer's job
is downsized and he/she starts making less
money and the recalculated amount owed
to the power company goes up to $200. The
customer cannot afford the new payment and
comes to an "arrangement" with the power
company that as long as they are paying in

good faith a reasonable amount, the company will continue to provide power and not shut off their electricity. Of course, there will be some unfortunate consequences. There will be additional fees for late payments and there will be interest charged on unpaid balances. Furthermore, the company requires that each year, the customer increase the amount paid, so the deficit will not grow as fast. The customer agrees. So for the next year, the customer pays $100 a month, thus getting behind at the rate of $100 a month plus the additional fees. At the end of the year the customer has an outstanding balance of $1800. This figure includes the actual balance plus fees and interest. The following year the recalculated amount goes to $225 and the customer agrees to increase his payment by 50 percent, a rather substantial amount. So now they are paying $150 a month and thus getting behind at a slower rate than the previous year. Thus, this year after all fees and penalties and interest are included, they actually did better than the previous year as their deficit this year is only $1500, a reduction of 17 percent from the previous year. The following year they make a very similar arrangement with the power company, increasing their monthly payment so that the deficit decreases again. When they explain to their friends what is happening, they claim success in that they are reducing the amount of increase in their personal debt by a significant amount each year. As long as they continue to do better each year things will get better and they will be okay!

Have you recognized the flaws in the logic of the consumer in the previous paragraph? Fact of the matter is, if they continue in the same manner and decrease their rate of increased debt, things will continue to get worse and worse and worse. Admittedly, things will get worse at a slower rate, but they will *never* get better as long as they follow this plan! (Sound familiar?) Getting behind at a slower pace is still getting behind and will never include catching up. And so our government tries to convince us that the rate of deficit spending decreases means that they are doing a good thing and helping our economy. They are as wrong as wrong can be.

Deficit reduction not only is not the answer, it actually is a bad bad bad thing. Growing our debt at a slower rate is still growing our debt and can only be a failed strategy. And remember, this is just the tip of the iceberg! Remember the "M", "B", "T" words? I could write an entire book recounting the absurdly inaccurate notions involving how our legislators confuse or use inaccurately the concepts of how a million or billion or trillion dollars impacts the budget. Think about this: If you earned $100,000 a year, it would take you ten years to earn a **m**illion dollars, and it would take you 10,000 years to earn a **b**illion dollars, and it would take you 10 million years to earn a **t**rillion dollars. Consider this: if you earned a dollar a second it would take about twelve days to earn a million dollars and thirty-two years to earn a billion dollars, and, 32,000 years to earn a trillion dollars. Another way to look at the same data is that when a person has lived a billion seconds he/she will be about 32 years old. How old are you in seconds?

Then there is the notion of interest on the

debt. Interest on the national debt is the single biggest item in the debt and like the story about the power company even if it gets worse at a slower rate, it still gets worse! Unlike the story of the power company, the rate that things are getting worse is not slowing down, and, even if it were, it would be like trying to empty the ocean with a cup rather than a spoon. One is better than the other is, but neither have a chance for success. The simple fact of the matter is that our government has acted in a totally incompetent and reckless manner and we, the people, are paying the price for their incompetence. Furthermore, it is clear to me that the incompetence of the past is an accurate predictor of the incompetence of the future. As long as we depend on incompetent legislators to try to do a job they are unable to do, we might as well ask our mechanics to perform heart surgery, for there is equal likelihood that the outcome will be successful. That is, the likelihood is zero. Add to the previously described problem the problems associated with how states and cities are dealing with their debt and the overwhelming problem becomes even worse. Everybody is talking about it, but when they try to find a solution, they are doomed to failure because they just do not have the mathematical intellect to properly attack the problem. You need to understand that by "mathematical intellect" I do not just mean computation, I also include reasoning, logic, and use of symbols in problem solving techniques. Mathematics is a way of thinking. Mathematics includes processing information in a manner that is just unique to the field of study. I assume that virtually everyone who reads this has heard the term *exponential growth* and probably has a notion as to what it means, but I also assume that only a very few really understand its impact on budgetary matters. The notion of cumulative compound interest even stagers the mind of those educated in financial analysis. Do I think that those senators and house members have the understanding necessary to make the decisions they are attempting to make? In a word: NO! But it saddens me to the core that they somehow believe that they do. There is no doubt in my mind that as long as we try to repeat the past we are doomed to failure. When you are doing something wrong, doing it repeatedly is not somehow going to make it right. Remember, the title of this book includes "common sense" and in my mind, it is only common sense that more of the same bad policies will result more in the same bad results. Even worse is that there is no hope for better decisions if the same uninformed incapable persons continue to try to do it better. Politicians that are not mathematicians cannot do the job of fixing the budget. Politicians who display an absolute refusal to accept that they are not capable of doing a job that has to be done are displaying inexcusable ignorance that could even be called malicious. Who do they think they are that they can continue to flaunt their power even as it becomes clearer how ineffective they are? Why do we let this continue? I will tell you why. The system is ingrained into our society and change cannot and will not happen as long as we are willing to accept this level of incompetence, and we will continue to accept this level of incompetence until someone somehow has the nerve, the determination, the guts and the power to create change. The system is so dysfunctional that it cannot be fixed. It can only be replaced by people who have the sense to recognize what they can, cannot do, and then will allow those who do know how to solve the problem to get to work and do it. Those who got us into these problems (Senators and members of the House of Representatives) are not going to get us out of these problems. More of the same is not the answer. A friend of mine claimed to have had the following conversation with a new car salesperson:

> Sales person: "I will sell you this car for less than we paid for it! I will show you our invoice and you are going to get it for less than we got it!" Friend: "That doesn't make sense. How can you make money by selling a car for less than you paid for it?" Sales person: (With a straight face, even!): "Volume!"

He (or she) should be in congress! The argument made here makes as much sense as the arguments that I hear most Sunday mornings on *Meet the Press* or *Face the Nation* or *Fox News Sunday* or *This Week with Christiane Amanpour* when our politicians say things that are just more of the same that got us into these problems to start with. The really hard news, to me, is that these are our elected officials—most of whom are sincere and dedicated, but somehow or another have convinced themselves that the 30-second news bite and saying the things that people want to hear but have no notion as to how to make these ideas come to fruition. Politicians should not be doing brain surgery or rebuilding a transmission or piloting an F-14 or fixing a budget! They are equally poorly trained to do any of these things! Just as they do not have the medical training to perform surgery, so also they do not have the mathematical skills to comprehend the problems involved with building a budget. No one disagrees that we do not want an untrained novice to do the first, how come we cannot grasp that it is equally true that we do not want an untrained novice to do the second?

Here is a problem that I recently submitted for publication in the calendar section of the *Mathematics Teacher*.

Twenty thousand patriotic millionaires decided to each give 50 percent of their savings to help reduce the national debt. Upon hearing of their generosity, a trillionaire decided to match the gifts. What percentage of her savings did she need to give to match the gift?

I sent this problem to my son who has his PhD in Physics and teaches at the college level. He commented on how important it is in a science class to help his students understand large numbers. Physicists deal with such things as the speed of light (which is a little more than 186 thousand miles per **second**) or the distance to the closest star. The closest star to the earth is actually the sun (about 93 million miles). The next closest star is more than 63,000 times further, or approximately 4.4 light years away! My son went on to say that he sometimes talks with his students about how to visualize large numbers. One example he uses is that large college football stadiums can hold approximately 100,000 people. Put 10 of those stadiums side by side and you have a million people. For many people, that is about as large as they can "visualize." But, to take it a step further, if you take 1000 of those groups of 10 stadiums, you would then have room for a billion people! And, of course, to take it to an extreme (as if we have not already done that) if you take 1000 of those groups of 1000 groups of 10 stadiums, you could hold a trillion people! But, since the entire population of the earth is dramatically less than a trillion, it is a moot point! As an addendum to the problem, I asked how these gifts would impact the national debt. That is another good question to think about. The few seconds it would take for me to state what the national debt really is are long enough to make the figure inaccurate! The national debt is changing by about $1,200 every second, which translates into about $77,000 each minute and about $4.6 million an hour. As a mathematician, I dislike the word "about" when giving an "answer" to a question, but in this case, it must be used.

The changes are occurring so fast and the amounts are fluctuating so much that approximations are the only reasonable way to describe them. Yet, those approximations must fall within reasonable parameters, and there are disagreements about how "close" one has to be to be considered reasonably accurate. So, I provide the disclaimer that these figures are my best guesses that may vary from other person's calculations. But, I am confident that they are "reasonably close!"

One last example: Suppose we were able to convince the ten richest people in the United States to donate their entire fortune to pay off the national debt. That would include such people as Bill Gates, Warren Buffett, the Walton family, and Michael Bloomberg, among others. That would still leave us with about 98 percent of the debt to deal with. And, of course, it would still be growing! I wish there were a way to make these examples required reading for all those folks who have something to do with budgetary matters. If it were, I doubt that they would be spending hours, days, and weeks arguing about spending cuts and tax revenues that are trivial as compared to the totality of the budget itself! We have all heard the tongue in cheek phrase "A million dollars here and another million dollars there, and pretty soon we are talking about real money." Well, when it comes to the national debt, maybe not so much! These examples of extreme innumeracy show why it is that the present system is so very broken that we cannot expect significant change with the people in charge now. God bless them... they are like brain surgeons trying to fix a transmission. No matter how smart, dedicated, and sincere they are, they just do not have the tools to do the job. I can hear the naysayers now saying that those who are working on the budget are economists who actually do have the mathematical training necessary to do the job. Well, that is *sort of* true. But, I guess that must also mean that it is *sort of* false. It is! The economists who are working on the budget report to the Senators and House members. They are advisers, not decision makers. As long as the process of deciding budgetary matters is the same as it is now, it is my belief that the system is self-defeating. It will not work; it cannot work, as long as the process is as it is now! Remember, if you still have any doubts that those who are in charge can really get us out of this mess, that it was the very same people working within the very same system that got us to where we are now! Do we really expect the people that made the decisions that got us here to get us elsewhere? I do not know precisely what the outcome will be if the budget crisis is actually handed over to mathematicians to solve, but I am confident that at least the five following problems will have to be considered:

1) The specific procedure as to how the budget decisions are made will have to change. We can no longer rely on the procedures that got us into this mess. They have not worked up till now, and they will not work in the future. Without radical change in the mechanics, there is no hope for radical change in the outcomes. And, radical change is what is needed. Members of

the House and Senate have enough to do without attempting to do precisely what they are unqualified to do: that is, fix the budget process. Turn the process over to people who know what they are doing and let them do it!

2) Eliminating waste and duplication will make the most significant difference in the current debt circumstances. Just by streamlining programs, the government can save more money than would be saved by raising taxes and cutting social programs. Waste is different from duplication and duplication is different from waste. Both issues must be addressed.

3) Besides the issues of waste and duplication, the budget process must address unnecessary spending! Downsizing the spending means making decisions about eliminating "pork" and other self-serving budget items that have been a mainstay of the present process. It is clear to me, and I would

guess it is clear to many, if not most, who have studied this problem that the "games" associated with getting specific spending projects attached to other major bills must be stopped! These are loopholes in the system that were created by politicians for their own benefit and have been perpetuated by those same politicians for decades! It is as wrong as wrong can be! The thought that those same politicians would work towards a better solution is laughable! Talk about the fox guarding the henhouse! That is almost a perfect analogy!

4) Just as there is waste, inefficiency, and duplication in the spending process, so are there waste, inefficiency, and duplication in the way our government collects money. That is, the tax system is, as I like to say, as broken as broken can be. I believe the problem is 70 percent spending and 30 percent revenue. While those numbers are "rough" estimates, they are assuredly

close enough to demonstrate that both sides of the equation need transformation. Before the government needs to make any decisions about raising or lowering tax rates, they must first address the unbelievably bizarre tax laws that are currently on the books. How many stories have we heard about how even the "experts" in the field come to different conclusions? Take your taxes to seven different accountants and give them all the same information and chances are you will owe seven different amounts to the state and federal government. It is so unnecessarily complicated that it defies any common sense at all! Broken? You had better believe it! And, does anyone out there think the same people who inherited and passed on this crazy system are the same ones that we want to entrust to make it better? Seems very unlikely to me! If you want to go on line and order a copy of the IRS codes that are currently in use, you can get the over 20-volume set for a little less than $1000. I feel very confident when I say that not one member of congress has read the code in its entirety, and to presume that any one of them understands the subtleties of the code is laughable. The basic structure of how these revisions to the tax code are made must be changed for there to be any hope of significant progress. The people who have been in charge have failed miserably. It is time for a radical restructuring of the system.

5) Finally, the spending cuts must start at home. Consider all of those millionaires and multi-millionaires who are in the House and Senate. The salaries they receive are an incredibly small part of the costs involved. The "fringe benefits" of being a member of congress are unbelievable. First, in order to get the seat they "won" in an election, they must have been filthy rich to start with. If it were common

knowledge just how much "extras" they each get because of their job, there would (should) be an outrage. Again, does anyone think that they are going to take any of those extras away from themselves? Of course not! I challenge one or more of the major news networks to do some real investigative reporting and uncover the shameful ways that our elected officials are spending tax dollars. I promise you this: you will be outraged when it is all put into a concise format. The rich get richer at the expense of the common citizens. To say that is unfair is a huge understatement. I have heard it said that with all its problems and faults, and as bad as it is, our system of government is still the best that exists. Well isn't that damning the system with false praise? Instead of looking at the second part of that sentence "it is still the best that exists," let's consider the first part about "all of its problems and faults." Are we really willing to accept a horribly bad system just because a better one doesn't currently exist? I sure hope not! I guess if that were the only alternative, maybe the answer would be yes, but it is not the only alternative. We also have the opportunity to take this system of government and make it better! Let us not settle for "good enough," when "good enough" has so very many problems!

PART II

PICK ONE OR TWO OR THREE OR. . .?

I must make one thing abundantly clear before I list the ten problems with living in America. I am so very proud to be an American. I am not, in any way, berating this wonderful country or finding fault with the glorious life that I have been blessed to live. My goal, here is to say that in this wonderful world that we live there are problems. And, those problems need to be addressed. Moreover, it will make a difference just how we do that. I believe that many (most?) people wish to leave the world in some way knowing that they did something good, thoughtful, productive, or meaningful and that we were able to make a difference in someone's life in a positive manner. However, many people, myself included, "talk the talk" better than we "walk the walk." But there are so many people who graciously do both, often behind the scenes in a manner that is unheralded and possibly even unnoticed. Very few people are going to be memorialized on national TV when they die and that is fine. There are thousands and thousands and thousands of the most wonderful people in the world who live lives that they are proud of and who die unbeknownst to the world except for those few folks that knew them well. My beloved Mom was such a person. She was one of those folks that we think of when we hear the phrase "the salt of the earth." She lived into her 90s, and it is not my intention of going on and on (though I could) about how grand of a person she was. She knew she was dying and we talked on her deathbed. She said that it appeared that her time was near and that death was eminent. Yes, we both knew that was the case. She said that she was glad that she had lived a good life and that she loved her children, grandchildren, great grandchildren, and that she modestly thought she had helped them to become the good people that they were. She had no regrets. She was proud of the life she had lived, and died a happy person. We should all be so lucky! I do not look forward to dying, but I do hope that when my time comes I will feel that I did right by those I loved and those who loved me and that someone somewhere is living a better life because I spent some time on this planet.

Therefore, that is, in part, what motivates me to write this book. In Part Two of this book I am going to list ten "Things to Think About" and maybe act on. I would love to find out which ones seem important and or significant to you, and I would love to find out from you which ones I omitted from my list that are indeed on your list! Who knows, maybe we will come up with a huge list of things to do to make this a better county to live in. Okay, here goes: Not in any special order, but here is my top-ten list of things to think about to make the world a better place. It is my deep hope that many of us, again, myself included, will pick one or two or three or...?

> 1) I believe there are two groups of people in this world who are more vulnerable than any others are: the very old and the very young. I would like to make it my mission to help someone in one or both of those categories on a regular basis. Precisely how I would do that is not the fodder for this book. However, some ideas would be to visit someone who just has no one to visit

them in a nursing home. Find a very poor family and support their children with books and food and clothing and love. In Part One of this book I presented four "big" problems that require a more "universal" solution. That is not the intent of this chapter. I will present the problem and leave the solution to you!

2) I believe there is a special place in Hell for those who maliciously and purposefully sexually abuse children. At least, I hope there is! There are multitudes of organizations that are dealing with this horrible crime. Most of them are faith-based organizations, but not all. Can I really go to sleep at night knowing that there is something I could do to make the world a safer place for an innocent child? I know that this list of ten "problems" is not going to get "solved" by me, but I want to be a part of the solution. I am listing ten here, and I don't even know as I sit here and type which ones I will make

part of my mission in life. I am not suggesting that I will respond to each of these in a way that I will feel good about, but I think that the process of writing about them and bringing them to the front of my thinking process rather than just sitting there in the back of my mind is a good start.

3) There are certain things that can be legislated and certain things that cannot be legislated. The top ten list that I am presenting here are all values that cannot be legislated. These focus on "pride," "compassion," commitment," "honesty," "dedication," and a "humanistic approach" to living. So, number three is simply to challenge you and to challenge me to find a cause. Decide on something that grabs at your heart and soul and make it a part of your life. Not necessarily a big part, but maybe so. Get involved in something that is bigger than you are. Live life with a purpose and determination, knowing that the day

will come when your opportunities on this earth are over and you too, just like me and everyone else, will want to ask the questions: "What have I done with this gift of life?" "What difference have I made?" and "Can I die with a smile on my face knowing that someone somewhere is better off because I have lived?"

4) There are some very controversial topics that well-meaning people of good character have differing opinions. The ones that come to my mind are abortion, the death penalty, the nation's emigration policies, same-sex marriage, the legalization of marijuana, and others as well. These are concerns of the heart as well as the mind. I believe that very good, honest, and dedicated people can differ in their opinions on these subjects. There are people who I love the most and who love me dearly that have dramatically differing views on some of these. So, my challenge to myself and to others

is to accept these people for who they are, embracing their strength of character as being more important than our philosophical or political or social differences. I need to become more tolerant of others heart-felt views and not condemn them because they differ with my heart-felt views. Agreeing with someone and respecting them can be very different perspectives. There are people who I intensely disagree with who I care about, respect, and love.

5) I am not sure if it is actually true that there have been a large increase in natural disasters or if the combination of better news coverage and the law of averages just seems to make it appear that way. But, as of the time I am writing this, there have been floods and huge fires and earthquakes and tornadoes and hurricanes that seem to have dominated the news. On the one hand, I am so very proud of the actions of our fellow citizens in their response

to these crises, and on the other hand I hurt because there is so much more that needs to be done. Thank heavens for the Red Cross and for FEMA (even with all its problems) and all of those many organizations that have stepped up to help. God bless you all! Here is one of those situations where many individuals can really have a huge impact on a problem. Each of us needs to find a way to do our part to help those who are suffering from these kinds of losses.

6) I am embarrassed to say that here I am, 66-years-old, and I have just now concluded that giving blood is an easy and good thing to do. It really is! Do it! It warms the heart and soul of the donor! I have also recently decided to declare myself as an organ donor. I don't know if this aging body will be of any value to anyone after my death, but I do know for sure that it will not be of any value to me! Just think, you and I can actually make it so that

someone can live a longer and fuller life just by leaving our dead body to be used for good!

7) I was born just as World War II was ending. My parents lived through it, but they were not much inclined to talk about it with my sister and me. I recall when I was in middle school and first heard the word Holocaust. I went home and asked questions, and to their credit, my parents did their best to explain what had happened in Nazi Germany during that time. I recall my response was to ask why we Americans did not stop it from happening. How could we live with ourselves knowing that such tragedies were going on? My parents replied that indeed we did do something: We fought a war. My mom's beloved brother, my Uncle Ted, had died in that war, along with thousands of others in an attempt to stop the carnage. I remember thinking that if there were a Holocaust going on during my adult

lifetime that I would be in the forefront of the fight against it. I believe there is one. I do not want to necessarily make a comparison to different tragedies or the circumstances surrounding those tragedies, but I do think that the fact that thousands of children go to bed hungry and many of them die every day that we are indeed living during a time that will be some day looked at and my grandchildren will ask the same questions of me that I asked of my parents. "Why did you not do something?" How can we stand by and allow innocent children to die when there really is enough food to feed everyone? We are so very blessed in this country, but there are too many who are not a part of that prosperity.

8) *Adversarial* is a good word used to describe certain aspects of our world, but not others. I must admit, I am a *Court TV* junkie! I love *Law and Order* and *In Session* and growing up *Perry Mason* was one of my favorites.

I learned, among other things, that defense attorneys and prosecuting attorneys were supposed to be in an adversarial relationship for the system to work. Each had the job of vigorously defending or prosecuting and on opposite sides of the isle they were often argumentative and caustic with one another. I wish it could work differently, but it does seem to be a system that that has survived the test of time. Yes, it has its problems, but for the purposes defined, it works. However, I cannot think of any other structure where purposefully creating an adversarial relationship is a positive thing. The Republicans and Democrats have taken the adversarial system and put it on steroids. And, I would say, much to the detriment of our country. They are so busy arguing for or against the party line that little, if anything, is done. Clearly, it is a good thing to have differences of opinions and to vigorously defend your position, but the government has set the standard for poor relationship building! I believe the primary reason this has happened is because we, the voters, have allowed it to happen. So, what to do? I am stating here and now that I will never again vote for a candidate whose message is one of cutting down his/her opponent. Only someone who is willing to run on a positive up beat platform will ever get my vote. If enough of us do that, this adversarial system that is on steroids will fall and maybe our government will start to get something done in a cooperative rather than adversarial manner.

9) I have recently become much more aware of persons with special needs because a dear friend had a ruptured brain aneurysm and stroke. For a long time she was in a wheel chair and then able to walk with a cane, with minimal use of her right side. Her speech was impacted and if you did

not know better, one might look at her and "wonder" about her abilities and intellect. She does not "look normal." She is! She has her PhD and her mind is functioning like the college professor she has been. Yet, she has a long way to go before she will have recovered from this disaster in her life. Thankfully, she is on the road to recovery. We don't know how much of her old self she will be able to reclaim, but we are all so very grateful for the help she has received from friends and doctors and physical therapists and most of all, from her own determination to become the best person she can be. She is my hero. I couldn't be more proud of her. She and I have both grown in our awareness of people with special needs. Most of us are so very lucky to not be "disabled." When I consider the number of children and adults who are blind or have Cerebral Palsy or have been badly hurt in an accident or suffer from extreme emotional distress or extreme physical disabilities I do think of the phrase, "there, but for the grace of God, go I." So, my point is this: these folks have been dealt the most difficult of hands. It is incumbent upon me to do what I can do to improve their lot in life. I am just talking about basic kindnesses and overt acts of compassion. If indeed a large number of people were to take on that attitude, it would make the world a better place.

10) I am in reasonably good shape financially. I am retired and live comfortably on my pension and social security. I don't live extravagantly and there are some toys out there that I would love to buy and probably could, but it seems irresponsible to me. My point is this: while not rich, neither am I poor. And, I guess it would be safe to say that I am closer to Upper Middle Class than Lower Middle Class. I am neither bragging nor complaining, just stating a fact. Now, more importantly

is to consider why I am stating this fact. There is a phrase, from *The Gospel According to Luke*, chapter 12 that goes something like this: "Those to whom much is given, much is expected." The word *much* is certainly a relative term, and in many ways it applies to many people who might not at first believe that this is referring to them. And note, the word *much* is used twice in that quote, and in each case it is a relative term. How much is much? And the word *expected* in this quote is also up to interpretation. I feel very strongly that the self-expectation of giving from ones heart and wealth means so much more than the gifts of money. My most precious commodity is time, and I am guessing that many would concur that their most precious commodity is time. To give of my resources includes my money and my time and my energy and my love and my compassion. Throwing money at a cause is often a very helpful, but not satisfactory solution. In this world that we live in today there is no shortage of causes to tug at our hearts and pocketbooks. Pick one or two or three or…

PART III

IN CONCLUSION...

It takes two things to happen for a good idea to come into fruition. First of all, it must in fact be a good idea. If any of the ideas presented in the preceding chapters is or is not a good idea is certainly up for debate. Of course, I believe they are all good ideas, but I would guess that I am in a minority. However, it would certainly surprise me if the readers of this book don't find one or more ideas that they can resonate with. In fact, it is hard for me to believe that the great majority of readers will not find some new information in this book that they could get behind and support with enthusiasm. The problem as I see it is that most of us (myself included) are not in positions of power nor do we have the influence to take the good idea and make it work. That indeed is the second of the two things that must happen for a good idea to be acted upon. Someone with influence and/or power must make this his or her mission. Is there someone out there with power who really thinks that one or more of these "common sense" solutions really is something that will work? I am virtually 100 percent sure that there are many folks who will be moved or influenced with one or more of these solutions, but I am not so sure that in fact there will be anyone who can actually make it happen who will read this. That is where my final common sense solution comes into play. And, I would guess to no one's surprise, it is a mathematical solution. I believe that the best way (possibly the only way) for any of these solutions to actually come to be acted upon is if there is a groundswell of pressure placed upon those who actually do have the influence and power to make it happen. If you think you are powerless to help that happen, you are wrong. Listen to the mathematics and I think you will agree that this can happen and each one of us is equally empowered to take the steps necessary to put the process in place. Almost all of us have heard of the "Ponzi Scheme." One of the largest Ponzi Schemes was perpetuated by Bernard Madoff and was in the news so much that the term Ponzi scheme came to be associated with him. A well-conceived Ponzi scheme, like many other frauds works, at least in part, because of a mathematical concept called exponential growth. The good news is that exponential growth can be used for good as well as for bad reasons. Basically, it works like this: Two or three or more people get it started by telling a small number more who are then instructed to tell a small number more who then continue the process until a huge population is involved. Sound complicated? It is not nearly as bad as it might sound. For the most part, pyramid schemes, or Ponzi Schemes or multilevel marketing or chain letters are illegal and are set up for profit for a few at the expense of the masses. Only if you are on one of the two or three top levels of one of these schemes can it be financially beneficial. But, what is also true is that the mathematical principles that are abused with all of these various schemes can be used effectively and positively in an attempt to communicate information to a large number of people in a quick manner. For instance, if just 10 people who are reading this page decide that what they have read deserves to be passed on to 10 more people, and then those 100 people (10 times 10) also decide to pass this information on to 10 friends for a total of the original 10 plus the next level of 100 plus the next level of 1000 for a grand total of 1110 with just three levels! Do this just three more levels and more than one million people will be buzzing about a common idea! This is called exponential growth and has amazing results especially when it grows one or two more levels. Literally, within weeks, the entire population of the United States could potentially have had the opportunity to be contacted. Yes, this is a form or a chain letter or pyramid scheme, but it has the one significant difference in that there is no money being promised or passed around and there is no one small group of people at the top of the pyramid who are "winning" at the expense of all the others on the lower level! It really is a win-win situation. If indeed someone is contacted who does not agree that this needs to be passed forward that is fine. The process will continue as long as some, if not all, of the participants keep the communication moving. The computer, and more specifically the internet, has changed the way we live in so many ways. All of a sudden the way presidents are elected, or sports and news is communicated, or the way children communicate with their parents and their friends, or the word is spread about innovative concepts and ideas is a function of how well the internet is used. To say it is phenomenal is a huge understatement. Styles of communication are changing so rapidly that it would be silly to even try to guess what the processes may look like twenty years from now, as compared to twenty years ago. Or, for that matter, as compared to today. Someone is going to come up with something that no one has thought of up till then and the process that we use now will look as outdated and archaic as can be! We are not in the "modern age" when it comes to science and technology. In fact, I believe that 20 years from now folks will look back at these days with a silly grin on their face as they think about how outmoded and outdated and how uncomplicated our sources of electronics were then. We have what we have, and we are who we are, and those of us that use what is available are those who will be able to do the best that can be done with the tools that are at our disposal.

Addendum to the Covenant
Community School (CCS) Concept

Of all of the common sense solutions presented in this book, this is the one that I feel personally best prepared to present. I am a retired teacher who spent forty-two years in the classroom. I was fortunate to have taught in a school that embraced the basic concepts of the CCS. I have participated in a school that works. I know that it can happen. However, I also realize that this reform movement will not come to fruition unless enough people read about it and believe in it. It does seem to me that there is no down side to following this plan. It is a win-win situation for students and teachers and administrators and parents. The costs of implementing a CCS will be trivial compared to the multitude of other options that have been made available. I believe this can happen! I believe it should happen! Will it happen? I don't know! But I do know that the only possibility it has of happening is that it be presented and then we see where it goes. I have done what I wanted to do. Now, if you have read this and believe that it has merit, it is your turn to stand up and be counted. I ask you to act accordingly.

Comments, suggestions, questions, and criticisms are welcomed and encouraged. Please use the email address and website address found on the back cover. Thank you.

APPENDIX

Covenant Community School
Application Form

Directions: Please read and study the covenant statements 1 - 5 carefully. If you find these statements to be ones that you wish to embrace, then write a short statement in the space provided indicating your desire to become a member of the Covenant Community School. When you are finished, sign the statement in the presence of a witness who must be a parent, guardian, or faculty member of the school to which you are applying. If you have any questions, please call 555-1221 or stop by the counselor's office.

1) I will not participate in disruptive behavior in any setting connected to the Covenant Community School.

2) I will be a positive participant in classroom activities, respecting the rights of all others in the community.

3) I will treat others as I expect others to treat

me: with fairness, compassion, dignity and respect.

4) I will accept responsibility for my own actions.

5) I will apply myself toward solid academic performance.

In this space (continue on back if you need more room) indicate your purpose for applying to this CCS.

Signed _____ Date _____

Witness _____ Date _____

REFERENCES

Gross, Ronald and Beatrice. (1985). *The Great School Debate. Which way for American education?* New York: Simon and Shuster.

Heath, Douglas H. (1984). *Schools of Hope.* San Francisco: Jossey-Bass.

Kopp, Sheldon. (1972). *If you meet the Buddha on the road, kill him.* New York: Bantam Books.

Lieberman, Myron. (1989). *Privatization and Educational Choice.* New York: St. Martin's Press.

National Research Council. (1989). *Everyone counts: A report to the nation on the future of mathematics education (1989).* Washington D.C.: National Academy Press (Author).

The National Commission on Excellence in Education. (1983). *A nation at risk: The imperative for educational reform.,* April 1983. Washington D.C.: (p. 201).

Sarason, Seymour B. (1990). *The predictable failure of educational reform.* San Francisco: Jossey-Bass Publishers.

Toch, Thomas. (1991). *In the Name of Excellence:*

The Struggle to reform the nation's schools, Why it's failing, and what should be done. Oxford: Oxford University Press.

About the Author

Dick Forringer received his Bachelors Degree from Kent State University, majoring in mathematics and he earned his Masters in Education from Fordham University. He retired after 42 years as a teacher and administrator at Durham Academy, in Durham, North Carolina. He is a recipient of the F. Robertson Hershey Distinguished Faculty award and the Brumley Excellence in Teaching award. Dick has had three feature articles published in *The Mathematics Teacher*, and has just completed a workbook designed as a supplementary text for an Algebra 1 course.

The author is very interested in hearing reader responses to this book. Please send email to: forringer@cssolutions.info or visit the web site http://cssolutions.info.

Thank you!